Football's All-Time Greats

DEFENSIVE LINEMEN

JOSH LEVENTHAL

WORLD BOOK

BOLT

This World Book edition of *Defensive Linemen*
is published by agreement between
Black Rabbit Books and World Book, Inc.
© 2017 Black Rabbit Books,
2140 Howard Dr. West,
North Mankato, MN 56003 U.S.A.
World Book, Inc.,
180 North LaSalle St., Suite 900,
Chicago, IL 60601 U.S.A.

Design and Production by Michael Sellner
Photo Research by Rhonda Milbrett

Library of Congress Control Number: 2015954845

HC ISBN: 978-0-7166-9637-7   PB ISBN: 978-0-7166-9638-4

Printed in the United States at CG Book Printers,
North Mankato, Minnesota, 56003. PO #1796 4/16

Image Credits
AP Images: ASSOCIATED
PRESS, Back Cover, 1, 12, 18; Jim
Mahoney, 20 (right); Matt Ludtke, 29; Matt
Patterson, 26; Matt Slocum, 4–5; NFL Photos,
21 (left); NFL, 21 (middle and right); Paul Spinelli,
19 (top), 20 (left); Pro Football Hall of Fame, 9;
Stephan Savoia, 23; Tom DiPace, 20 (middle); Vernon
Biever, 15; Corbis: Bettmann, 11; David Richard/AP,
Cover; Getty: George Gojkovich, 24; Hy Peskin, 10;
Shutterstock: EKS, 3, 6–7, 20–21; enterlinedesign, 28–29
(ball); Orgus88, 19 (bottom); Svyatoslav Aleksandrov,
31; VitaminCo, 32; USA Today: Kevin Jairaj, 6; Mal-
colm Emmons, 16; Troy Taormina, 6–7, 7
Every effort has been made to contact copyright
holders for material reproduced in this
book. Any omissions will be rectified in
subsequent printings if notice is
given to the publisher.

Contents

CHAPTER 1

Stopping the Ball

The defensive lineman looks at the player facing him. The quarterback yells, "hike!" The two players crash into each other. The defensive lineman pushes past. He races toward the quarterback. It's a sack!

A DEFENSIVE LINEMAN'S STANCE

one or two
**hands on
the ground**

**ready to
spring up**

Step 1

Step 2

get to
the ball

push
past other
player

Step 3

CHAPTER 2

Linemen

from 1920 to 1965

Defensive linemen are tough and strong. Their job is to stop players carrying the ball. They also stop quarterbacks from passing.

Years ago, linemen played **offense** and **defense**. In the 1950s, their jobs changed. Linemen played only one part.

Bob Lilly

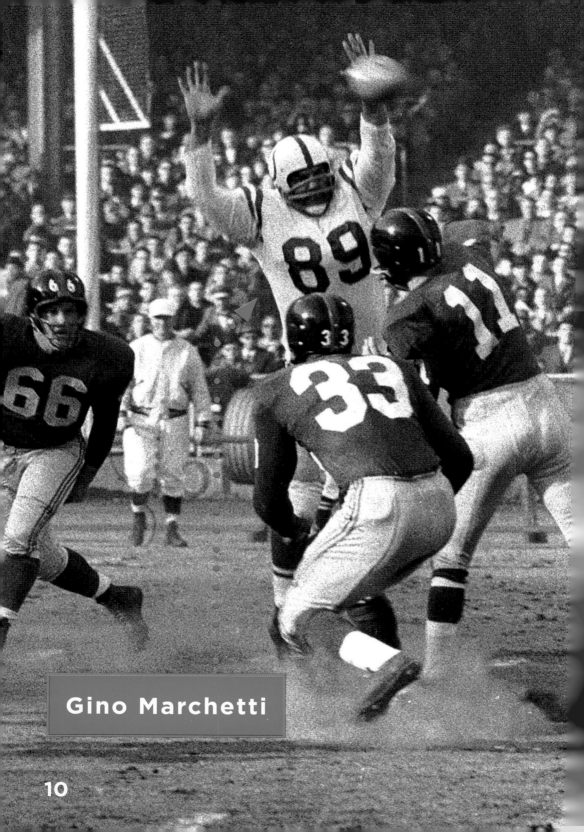

Gino Marchetti

Cal Hubbard and Gino Marchetti

Cal Hubbard was known for his size and speed. With his help, the Packers won three straight championships.

Gino Marchetti was a feared lineman. He was excellent at stopping the ball. Many people say he was the best **defensive end** (DE) in history.

Doug Atkins

Doug Atkins and Bob Lilly

Doug Atkins played 205 games at DE. He was tall and strong. He would jump over players to get to the ball.

Bob Lilly played his whole career with the Cowboys. Teams put two or three blockers on Lilly. But they couldn't slow him down.

Linemen in the Hall of Fame
(through 2015)

two-way players (players who played both offense and defense)	offensive linemen	defensive linemen
16	42	36

CHAPTER 3

Linemen

from 1966 to 1999

In the 1960s and 1970s, many teams had powerful defensive lines. The Rams had the "Fearsome Foursome." The Vikings had the "Purple People Eaters." The Steelers had the "Steel Curtain." These teams had great defensive linemen.

Alan Page

Merlin Olsen

Merlin Olsen and Alan Page

Merlin Olsen was a **defensive tackle** (DT) for the Rams. He played in 14 **Pro Bowls**. Olsen never missed a game in his career.

Alan Page was DT for the Vikings. He went after ball carriers. He didn't wait for them to come to him. Page is the only defensive lineman to win the Most Valuable Player (MVP) award.

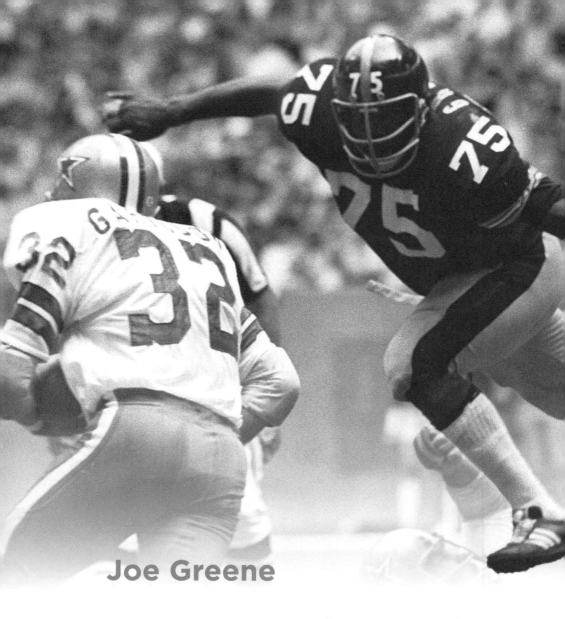

Joe Greene

Joe Greene was quick, strong, and played with feeling. He earned the nickname "Mean Joe." Greene made 190 tackles in one season alone.

Reggie White

Reggie White was a powerhouse. He earned 13 trips to the Pro Bowl. His 198 career sacks are the second most of all time.

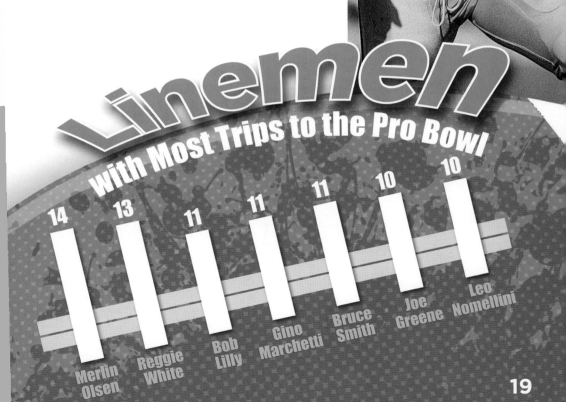

Linemen
with Most Trips to the Pro Bowl

14 — Merlin Olsen
13 — Reggie White
11 — Bob Lilly
11 — Gino Marchetti
11 — Bruce Smith
10 — Joe Greene
10 — Leo Nomellini

SIZE THEM UP

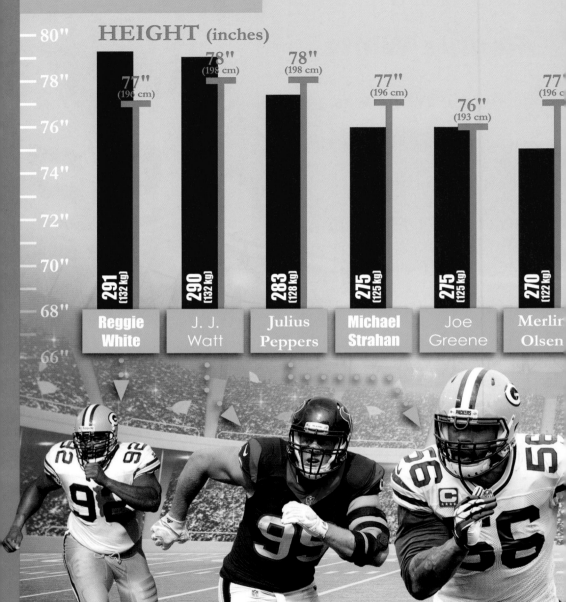

HEIGHT (inches)

77" (196 cm)	78" (198 cm)	78" (198 cm)	77" (196 cm)	76" (193 cm)	77" (196 c
291 [132 kg]	290 [132 kg]	283 [128 kg]	275 [125 kg]	275 [125 kg]	270 [122 kg]
Reggie White	J. J. Watt	Julius Peppers	Michael Strahan	Joe Greene	Merlin Olsen

WEIGHT
(pounds)

295
290
285
280
275
270
265
260
255
250
245
240
235
230
225

80"
(203 cm)

77"
(196 cm)

76"
(193 cm)

76"
(193 cm)

76"
(193 cm)

74"
(188 cm)

262
(119 kg)
Bruce Smith

260
(118 kg)
Bob Lilly

257
(117 kg)
Doug Atkins

253
(115 kg)
Cal Hubbard

245
(111 kg)
Alan Page

244
(111 kg)
Gino Marchetti

CHAPTER 4

Linemen

from 2000 to Today

Linemen are faster and bigger than ever. Since 2000, four linemen have made 20 sacks or more in a season. Defensive linemen are also **intercepting** more passes.

Michael Strahan

Most Sacks by a
Defensive
Lineman
in One Season
(1982-2015)

Michael
Strahan
2001
22.5

Mark
Gastinea
1984
22

Bruce Smith and Michael Strahan

Bruce Smith made 200 sacks in his career. He was strong. His strength helped him push past defenders to get to quarterbacks.

Michael Strahan made the most sacks in one season. He had 22.5 sacks in 2001. Strahan also led the NFL with 18.5 sacks in 2003.

ared llen 2011	Reggie White 1987	Chris Doleman 1989	J. J. Watt 2012 & 2014
22	21	21	20.5

J. J. Watt

Julius Peppers and J. J. Watt

Julius Peppers was named Defensive Rookie of the Year in 2002. Teams often put two or three defenders on him. But he still causes **fumbles**.

J. J. Watt was named Defensive Player of the Year in 2012, 2014, and 2015. He's the first player to make more than 20 sacks in two seasons.

Peppers started playing linebacker in 2015. But many people think he'll be remembered as a lineman.

Defending the Win

Linemen are a team's defensive front line. They must stop the ball. A great defensive line can win the game.

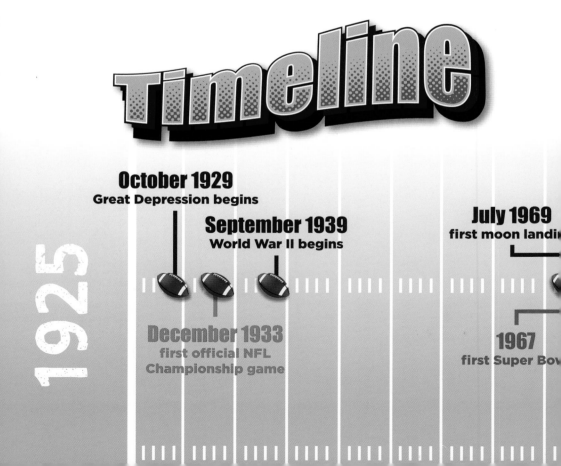

Timeline

1925

October 1929
Great Depression begins

September 1939
World War II begins

December 1933
first official NFL
Championship game

July 1969
first moon landi

1967
first Super Bow

Julius Peppers

1982
NFL starts
racking sacks.

1984
Mark Gastineau
of the Jets
has 22 sacks
in one season.

September 2001
terrorist attack on World
Trade Center and Pentagon

2001
Michael Strahan
sets
single-season
sack record
with 22.5.

2014
J. J. Watt
has more than
20 sacks for a
second season.

2015

defense (DEE-fens)—the players on a team who try to stop the other team from scoring

defensive end (dee-FEN-siv END)—a defensive lineman who lines up on the outside spots of a defensive line

defensive tackle (dee-FEN-siv TAK-uhl)—a defensive lineman who lines up on the inside spots of a defensive line

fumble (FUM-buhl)—a ball that is loose because a player failed to hold on to it

intercept (in-tur-SEPT)—to catch a pass made by the other team

offense (AW-fens)—the group of players in control of the ball trying to score points

Pro Bowl (PRO BOHL)—the all-star game of the NFL

sack (SAK)—a tackle of the quarterback before he passes, hands off, or crosses the line of scrimmage

BOOKS

Challen, Paul. *What Does a Lineman Do?* Football Smarts. New York: PowerKids Press, 2015.

Polzer, Tim. *Defense!* New York: Scholastic, 2011.

Scheff, Matt. *Superstars of the New York Giants.* Pro Sports Superstars. Mankato, MN: Amicus High Interest, 2014.

WEBSITES

Football: Defensive Formations
www.ducksters.com/sports/football/defensive_formations.php

Play Like a Pro! – Defensive Lineman Stance and Start
www.youtube.com/watch?v=_2iYpzwNxYQ

Pro Football Hall of Fame
www.profootballhof.com

INDEX